Shit Happens

Shit Happens
Implications of Physicalism in Satanic Philosophy

Damien Ba'al

Published by Skeptic

an imprint of HLA Publishing LLC

hlapublishing.com

ISBN: 978-0-9986198-3-5

Also by Damien Ba'al

The Satanic Narratives: A Modern Satanic Bible*

United Aspects of Satan: The Black Book

The Satanic Praxis: Living the Narratives

* Also available in Spanish

To the seekers of knowledge and wisdom, may you feast every day, yet always remain hungry for more.

Acknowledgements

Very special thanks to Wendy Ba'al for her love and support.

Thanks to Iris Shaw for the pentagram and flaming skull.

Thanks to Arcane Photography for cover photo.

Thanks to Tracey Pryor for the sigil of Baphomet.

Thanks to Khandnalie Barnes for all other sigils and symbols.

Thanks to Trig Kendrick for the title page art.

Contents

Prologue

This began as a new essay, but quickly expanded as time went on. It soon became apparent that Shit Happens was going to be quite long. At first, I considered an e-book like Disturbing Lack of Faith. After some thought, I decided to do more than that.

Many people prefer things in print. Even those who like e-books seem to appreciate compilations of material from the websites. United Aspects of Satan: The Black Book went over quite well. Therefore, I decided to put together the writings I have done since then.

The first essay here is Disturbing Lack of Faith, which I wrote 2013 to 2014. I released it as a short e-book. This will be its first time in print. It is my reasoning for not believing in gods and seeing faith as foolishness. It is primarily from the perspective of epistemology.

The next is the eponymous essay of the book. It is the longest one I have written to date. It was originally titled "Shit Happens: Implications of Materialism in Satanic Philosophy". However, I soon discovered that even highly intelligent, well-read people did not understand the word "materialism". I decided to go with "physicalism" instead.

People always seem to assume materialism is meant in an economic sense, even when the context is philosophy. In the essay, I explain the meaning of philosophical materialism. However, that does not help with people misunderstanding the title of the book.

The word "physicalism" does not have a common meaning outside of philosophy the way "materialism" does. It is more technically correct anyway. Physicalism is usually what is meant when people use "materialism" in the philosophical sense. "Materialism" has become the catch-all, categorical term in philosophy, but "physicalism" will not be misunderstood.

The essay goes over philosophical concepts related to a materialist worldview. There are philosophical problems between the materialist aspect of LaVey's philosophy, and other aspects, particularly those borrowed from Ayn Rand. My take on Satanism eliminates the tenuous pieces in favor of concepts that are in line with skepticism. As always, I do not shy away from my heretical ideas.

The next essay, "All in Your Head", is also new and deals with the subjective aspects of Satanism. The individualism of Satanism and the void left by a view of existential nihilism leave much up to the individual. It is about customizing one's subjective experience.

The remaining four essays are previously written material. I present them from oldest to newest. The abortion essay does have a little added to the end that is not on the website version. The "Free Speech Issues" essay was only a post on social media originally. I had it saved though, and was able to turn it into the short essay presented here.

From the beginning, I felt digging deeper into philosophy was the proper direction for Satanism. I only hinted at the depth of it in The Satanic Narratives, which was the right idea for a foundational book. I expand on many of the details here. This should make it clear that a more complete and properly reasoned philosophy is what the United Aspects of Satan is all about. Although you do not have to be a member to use it.

Taking an idea that is central to Satanism as originally envisioned, like materialism, but not ignoring it in other parts of the philosophy is critical, for me. That is the root of many of the differences between LaVey's philosophy and mine.

Why bother? The central ideas like materialism, individualism, and an Epicurean way of dealing with existential nihilism, to mention a few, are so very right. I am also entirely unable to even consider giving a half-hearted, fractional fuck about the old guard disliking it.

Either philosophy matters or it does not. If it does not, and you dislike spiritual bullshit as much as I do, then you really have nothing left. People will dogmatically continue to do as they have and believe what they wish, and that is fine. My preference is being philosophically consistent, and being the heretic that I am, I have never felt tied to any old baggage. I am far from alone in this. Here's to my fellow heretical Satanists!

Ave Satanas!

𝕬 𝕯𝖎𝖘𝖙𝖚𝖗𝖇𝖎𝖓𝖌 𝕷𝖆𝖈𝖐 𝖔𝖋 𝕱𝖆𝖎𝖙𝖍

Atheists of all sorts, me included, are entirely lacking in faith. The religious and faithful find this lack of faith quite disturbing. The concept of god is truly a ridiculous philosophical proposition. Faith is far from a virtue, and is in fact, foolishness and folly. Theistic religion is fading, faith is dying, and superstition is crumbling to dust. To hasten this demise, detailed herein, are the problems with gods and faith.

The question of whether or not any gods exist is, like any other question, one that should be approached with skepticism. By skepticism, I mean in a methodological sense, just like science. Saying that one must accept the existence of a deity on faith is an example of a logical fallacy called, "special pleading". That is where you require something, which is not required in other situations. In this case taking something on faith, or to put it another way, accepting it as truth without evidence, or even in spite of evidence, is different from how other things are approached. Normally to accept something as true, there must be some sort of evidence. Therefore, it is a fallacy to expect this question of the existence of gods to get this special sort of treatment.

Skepticism should never be confused with denialism. Skepticism means only accepting something as true if you have evidence. Without evidence, you have to consider it unknown. Denialism on the other hand, is the act of continuing to deny and doubt despite there being evidence. These are two very different things.

Evidence is the way to know something is true. There are two different kinds of evidence, which are usually used together. One type is logic or reason. This is the foundation of how we know things. It comes from our ability to think. Having any sort of discussion involves the use of reason. The other kind of evidence is empiricism, or empirical evidence. This is the raw data from science. It can be observations you make directly, or even data you discover indirectly.

Science is a certain kind of methodology for combining empirical data with reason. This method is how we come to know just about anything. With empirical data alone, without reason, you cannot make any conclusions about what you observe, or use it to make a model of reality. You even need reason to know that empirical data is an important part of knowing things. Without empirical data, you cannot know anything outside of your own mind. You can use logic and reason to figure out things that must be true based on axioms or mathematics, but to make conclusions about the natural world you must have information about that world. So in this way we can observe and experiment, apply reason to what we learn, and in so doing, come up with a useful model of reality.

There are two other ways you can know something. One of those is simply to make it up. An example of this would be fiction, like novels or movies. The other way is communication. Any communication though, is just the relaying of information that came from somewhere else. So while it is a way to know something, it is not an original source of knowledge. This leaves the mind as the only source of knowledge other than reason and empirical evidence. Therefore, if something did not come from reason or empirical evidence, it can only have come from a mind.

The heart of the matter is that there is no evidence for a god of any sort. There is no empirical data indicating such a being exists, and no logical arguments that stand up to scrutiny. So like anything else for which there is no evidence, there is no reason to think any gods exist. Without evidence, there is only one remaining way that we can even know about the concepts of all the different gods people have claimed throughout centuries. They had to have all been made up. The human mind is the only source of that knowledge unaccounted for.

At this point, some people might claim that we can only say that we do not know if some sort of god exists or not. However, there is not even evidence suggesting a god might exist. Therefore, we can at least be pretty sure that god does not exist.

While it is true that we cannot claim with absolute certainty that there are no gods, that is the case with a lot of other things as well. Many things that practically everyone thinks are mythological cannot be disproved. Unicorns, dragons, goblins, elves, leprechauns, and fairies are things, which cannot be disproved with absolute certainty. We do not think they exist because there is no reason to think so.

Throughout history, there have been many gods claimed to be real, and many people sincerely believed in them. However when these religions died off, everyone started accepting that they were mythological. There is no reason to think the gods of today are any different. This also shows a pattern that people have a tendency to invent gods.

If there are thousands of gods, which practically everyone agrees, are made up, then it is highly illogical to think that one particular god is an exception to that. You have primitive people who believed in all kinds of different magical things: they show a pattern of making up gods, there is no evidence at all of a god, and there is not even a way to know the concept other than making it up. Yet people believe that some particular god is real anyway, even though all reason says it is not. That seems to me like utter madness. A thing you cannot see, which performs magical acts, has no evidence, and was written about by people who show a pervasive pattern of making things up, and yet it is expected that we believe it. There is nothing else but god that people believe in under those circumstances. This is the absolute epitome of special pleading.

Some people might say that a particular holy book is evidence because it says god is real. Yet the reason stated we are to believe that, is because god inspired the writing. That is circular reasoning, and not a valid argument. There is also no way to verify the stories, and frequent contradictions can be found.

People may then ask how the earth, or people, or the universe, or any number of things came to be. Some of them might be science deniers, and the argument might be about physics, biochemistry, or evolution and natural selection. Or, they might just point out that there are gaps in the knowledge of science. They are essentially saying that because we do not know something, it must be this magical being they believe in. It boils down to "We do not know, therefore I know with absolute certainty". That is an argument from ignorance, which is a logical fallacy. This idea is also called "the god of the gaps". A gap in knowledge is a reason to find an answer, not a reason to invent one.

People might try to claim that miracles happen, or that god answers their prayers. However, a miracle is by definition an event that could not happen naturally or something that is impossible. Everything claimed to be miracles though, are things that could have just happened. Even if something were to happen which we could not explain, inserting god as the cause would be an argument from ignorance, just as in the above paragraph.

Prayers are much the same way. If god has a plan, then you are asking him to modify his plan, and change causality. He would also have known you would want this since the beginning of time, so if it was going to happen, it would already be in his plan. If it is not in the plan then it is not going to happen even If you ask. Therefore prayer not only does not qualify as evidence, it is entirely useless in regard to an omniscient being. Yet people believe in it regardless of outcome. If it happens, god heard them; if it does not then he works in mysterious ways, or has a plan. So clearly, it operates just like chance.

If you postulate a universe where there is no god, and things just happen, there is no way to differentiate it from the universe we live in. In both cases, things just happen as if nobody is controlling it. When good things happen, people thank god, even when we know the natural cause of the event, as if he allowed it to happen. Yet when bad things happen, they do not blame god, and think either it just happened, or make the "plan" excuse. So here again we see no evidence, and people just making excuses.

Some people might say you should believe anyway, just in case, much like Pascal did. The problem with that is that god would know you do not really believe, and you are faking it just in case. So, it really would not do any good. The next problem is that you have to decide which god. Many gods said to exist will punish you for believing in the wrong one. Believing in the wrong one is usually less favorable than not believing according to most mythological accounts.

One also must wonder why a god would want to be worshiped, or value gullible people who believe without evidence, over those who are more skeptical. It certainly seems improbable anyway, even without examining further. When you do examine it further, it seems even more improbable, since any god that exists is doing a very good job of hiding its existence.

People make all kinds of claims about what god wants. It is very interesting that their god tends to be in agreement with them on everything. It is a lot like god exists only in their minds. Any accounts of gods, or what they want, do not stand up to scrutiny, so we know their source is the human mind. It is also interesting that what they think, and want, very much fits with the times in which they were invented.

With modern believers, it does not matter which way they cherry-pick their holy book, their god always agrees. A more liberal Christian from Europe or the coastal areas of America will see god as very tolerant and loving. However, a Christian down in the Bible belt thinks god is primarily concerned with gays, abortion, and birth control. It is the same way with Muslims. In western countries they are usually all about peace, although there can be exceptions. In the very poor countries in the Middle East, and Africa they are much more likely to be militant. Anywhere the people happen to be more primitive and violent, so is their god; and they cherry-pick their holy book accordingly.

Since there is no evidence of any gods, if a god did exist, it is almost certainly concealing itself for some reason. A being that conceals its existence certainly does not want to be worshiped, nor have people perform any tasks for it. The most logical reason for concealing its existence would be to prevent knowledge of itself from altering human society. So, any god that did happen to exist almost certainly wants us to live as if there are no gods. Therefore, in the extremely unlikely event of some sort of god existing, the nonbeliever would be living the way it wanted while the believer would be doing the opposite.

Some people might say that religion has done a lot of good. However, it is not logical to believe in something because you think it would be good if it were true. You should only believe in something if it actually is true.

Religion has not done any good. The people who did these good deeds would have done them regardless. Religion has generally been harmful. It has not been the cause of the evil acts committed in its name, so much as it has had a negative influence on human society.

Some of my fellow atheists may be objecting at this point, saying that religion is the cause of all kinds of evil acts.

Therefore, I will endeavor to explain. Certainly none of them would object to my statement that religious people would have done good deeds without religion. Well, in both cases the reasoning is the same. People would have done terrible things anyway.

Religion is always the justification, and the details of the acts. If you notice, in the case of fundamentalism, the god agrees with the person. As there are no gods, clearly the person wanted to do these terrible acts anyway. You also cannot underestimate the power of brainwashing, and its frequent use in political movements. There is also the fact that all religious people would do terrible things if religion were the cause rather than the justification. The argument cuts both ways, because if religion did not cause the evil acts, it did not cause the good ones. Therefore, the religious cannot claim one without the other. The net result is that religion has been a negative influence, and a justification.

The worst thing about religion seems to be the organizational part. That is a big negative even when religion is not involved. Take Stalin's Communist movement for example. There was no religion involved, but you had people organized around some fanatical beliefs, and they did terrible things. Nationalism is another ideology like this. It is a group of people with fanatical beliefs, who cannot be reasoned with, who are willing to commit acts of violence.

Therefore, even though religion in general has been a negative influence, it is only the fundamentalist versions of it that continue to do great harm. While it is the fanaticism, and not the religion itself that is directly responsible, it is the religion that makes it hard to combat.

It is easier to fight a fundamentalist ideology when people agree it is a bad thing. However when it is done in the name of religion, it is hard to turn people against it, since they associate religion with good and morality. This is one of the negative influences religion has. Another is its politicization, where it is the justification to prevent certain groups from having equal rights, or to interfere with scientific education and advancement.

In conclusion, I would say that living with "a disturbing lack of faith" is the way to go. Not only is there no reason to believe any gods exist, but if one did, it would want you to think it did not. Religion also has a negative influence for the most part, and reducing this influence can only be a good thing. This is especially true in places where it mixes with politics. The more you think about the concept of god, the more outlandish an idea it seems. Eventually you reach a point where the question of god is not much of a question, and you do not understand how any rational person could believe in it. A lack of faith is a very good thing, and only the religious find it disturbing.

Shit Happens
Implications of Physicalism in Satanic Philosophy

The section labeled "Mental Models" is where the essay proper begins. First, I feel the need to preface it with explanations of what I mean by many of the terms. This will make it more accessible and cut down on confusion with people who may be less versed in philosophy and apt to get an unintended meaning from these terms.

When I use the word "materialism", I mean in a philosophical sense, and not an economic one. Materialism is a type of philosophical monism. In The Satanic Narratives, at the end of The Narrative of Lucifer, I put "dualism" in a list of concepts I rejected. I briefly mentioned rejecting not only ideas like afterlife and the soul, but also dualism of any kind. Monism means the mind is one thing, linked to the physical brain.

Materialism also is a rejection of the supernatural, and is usually taken as being synonymous with physicalism. In materialism, only the natural world exists, and mental processes are all a result of physical processes in the brain.

When I mention moral nihilism, I mean a position on meta-ethics that there is no objective source of morality. Nothing is intrinsically right or wrong. Meta-ethics is about 'what is', from a moral perspective, what exists, or what is an intrinsic moral property of the universe. "What is goodness" or "what is badness" would be questions in the realm of meta-ethics.

This is distinct from normative values. Normative values is about "what should you do". One can believe there is no intrinsic moral property in the universe, yet still have normative values about what should or should not be done, based on some criteria. Therefore, it is possible to have a strong sense of ethics and still be a moral nihilist. You can believe there is no such thing as goodness or badness, in an objective sense, intrinsic to the universe, yet still have some subjective basis for deciding what goodness should be.

These are also different from applied ethics or moral imperatives where one takes certain actions based on moral considerations. So one might believe the universe has no inherent moral property, yet may also see right and wrong from the basis of human wellbeing, and then use reason to arrive at a moral action based on that concept of right and wrong.

Therefore, moral nihilism has nothing to do with one's values and behaviors, and is only concerning what one believes is objectively inherent to the universe from a moral perspective.

When I get into existential nihilism, I mean that there is no intrinsic meaning or purpose in life. So in the absence of value, meaning, purpose, or external intentionality that could provide these things, each person must create their own meaning and purpose.

How one creates meaning and purpose is entirely subjective. It is up to each individual to determine that. Making the most of these choices is a major part of Satanic philosophy.

Mental Models

The mental model people have of reality and their place within it has greatly improved over time. However, even now the mental model people have is off in many ways. There are philosophies that have differing mental models, some more accepted than others. Some with more, and better, justifications for the different parts of their mental model of reality.

I take a different approach than many in Satanism do. That is because I am not willing to make the assumptions some others make. I am also not willing to take beliefs as axiomatic, when they clearly are not, just because other authorities seemingly do so.

I have an approach to reality that is vetted and generally accepted: scientific and philosophical skepticism. People do tend to selectively ignore them when they contradict certain beliefs they hold though. In addition, many people do not understand the inner workings of how we know things to begin with.

For many who would read this, the idea of not believing in the existence of things without evidence, is well accepted. A lot of Satanists are materialists. So like me, they do not believe in any deities, or any other supernatural entities.

Usually moral nihilism is fairly well accepted. Some may differ on how normative values are constructed, but as far as meta-ethics, tend not to believe in any objective source of morality. Some people do not understand it on that level though, even though that is essentially how they think of moral propositions.

Existential nihilism is a philosophy where people do not see the inner workings or all the implications, but generally understand they must make their own meaning and purpose. It can be taken further than people realize though.

Meaning and purpose of every sort are subjective or based on a particular situation. The same thing with which experiences hold what quantity of value, and what those values mean. It is up to the person experiencing it.

That stuff is all easier to understand and accept. I have touched on these topics a little in the past, and eventually plan to write a full-length book where I dig into them in detail. I bring them up here because they lead into the main topic.

Now I want to get into things that are not so easy to understand or accept, and have implications that overturn assumptions people make. They are part of the materialist worldview, but people do not typically realize that.

Luck and Chance

Who people are, what they accomplish, much of their perceived value, and many other aspects are an illusion of sorts. Luck and chance are just about everything. I am not even talking about arguments regarding free will and determinism at this point. I just mean things beyond control that result in that which people commonly accept as merit.

Luck and chance are words we use to refer to things that happened, which were not done with intention, or happened through processes with no intentionality. These happenings can be causes of other things, and nearly always are in the net of causal reality in which we live.

Take the genetics of a person for example. This would make up much or all of what we refer to as "nature" as opposed to "nurture". A person receives genes from parents, which in turn came from previous ancestors going all the way back to simple organisms that blurred the line between chemistry and biology.

How the genes express themselves and the traits people end up with are not a process we have any control over, or at least very little. The person who is the result of this certainly has no control over it, so how they end up has nothing to do with them.

Anything they got in this manner, that leads to anything attributed to merit, therefore is not really merit. No more than it is the fault of a person born with certain disabilities, that they have disabilities.

People also cannot control who their parents are, what resources their parents have, what country they are in, what is available to them, what lessons they are taught, what they are not taught, etc. This is everything we put under "nurture".

So if nature and nurture are nothing but happenstance, then what? People point to character and say that person could do this or do that. Where does this character come from? How do they know to do these things? Were these things learned? Were they born with this? It still falls under happenstance.

People who are not materialist can point to souls and other silliness like that. Of course, there is no evidence for such things. Therefore, that is not rational.

People talk about responsibility, strength, courage, and many other things. Sure, maybe in a colloquial sense, as applied to the day to day, these concepts make sense. However, as part of philosophy, as the criteria for who is good and deserving, it is nonsense.

It is nearly as ridiculous as the Abrahamic concept of being virtuous and good, therefore deserving. They believe god made all of reality, and knows how all events will unfold. Therefore, he made people to have the traits that would lead to whatever each one's given fate is.

They talk of free will, but there can be no free will in such a circumstance. Even if there could be, the creator god made all the characteristics of each person and designed their life circumstances. Therefore, this creator god is solely responsible for everything that happens.

It is the same way without a god. You just swap "God" for happenstance. Everything of nature and nurture are all ultimately the result of happenstance, therefore chance is the ultimate cause of everything and every outcome.

Many who stop having irrational beliefs about the supernatural and otherworldly realms continue to believe in personal attributes intrinsic to individuals. They do not believe in anything but the natural world, yet cling to concepts that are predicated on a spiritual essence of humanity, separate from material reality. The concepts themselves are natural, but without some element separate from the causal reality of the material world, their causes are saturated in happenstance.

The concept of "deserve" is more subjective than people think, and therefore should not carry the meaning it does with some. It means you should get something. "Should" is a value judgment. Even without taking the chance angle into consideration. When you do take it into consideration, it is a subjective value judgment based on the outcome of complex series of events that can all be traced back to chance happenings.

This idea people have of who they are and what a person is, and who each individual is, is colored by ideas where one's personhood is divorced from the material universe and causal reality. There is nothing outside of those things though, people included.

In LaVey's philosophy, humans are recognized as merely being animals. We are smarter, but just animals. However, the philosophy goes on to give us all sorts of attributes, which can only be the result of our brains, according to other parts of the philosophy.

I agree with all that, minus those attributes. We seem to have these attributes, but they are an illusion. It seems like we accomplished things all on our own, but what we used to accomplish them are the result of circumstances beyond our control.

Responsibility to the responsible? How did people become responsible? Genetically predisposed to prefer that? Taught to be that way? Alternatively, even if they learned it, what caused them to do that? It boils down to chance happenings. It certainly cannot be any innate quality of a person. That idea is not compatible with materialism where we are just part of the natural world.

We are smarter than other animals, and our brains create a much more complex subjective experience for us. This is what shapes our reality. It also lets us understand objective reality beyond our personal experience of life.

This quality of "deserving" and "merit" are used as a criteria for deciding a hierarchy of who is better than who. It determines who SHOULD get more resources, who has worth and who is worthless. It is held up as objective criteria for a value judgment, but requires some human essence divorced from the material universe.

In materialism, this all falls apart. That is because there is no human essence outside of the natural world. We may live as emergent entities, separated by layers of abstraction, but we are physical underneath. We are tiny stitches in the net of causal reality, made up of even smaller threads.

Is chance actually chance?

It probably is not. Chance appears to be chance due to the complexity of our universe. However, complexity just obfuscates the reality that the laws of physics determine what happens.

All the way down to the level of particles, everything obeys the laws of physics. Therefore, it would be possible to predict all outcomes, were it not for the complexity involved. In that way, there is no chance, no choice, no free will, and we are illusions created by complex brains that exist only because they increase survival to a great extent.

We are not separate from this process though, so it is not quite so simple. Our brains do sort of control things, it is just that they do so through the laws of physics. Therefore, our will and the particle interactions in our brain are one.

That is how there can sort of be free will in a way, but not really. There is the concept of emergence too, but again, that is still the result of physics.

We end up living in the illusion of free will, while knowing ultimately that it does not exist. The self is the center of our reality, it is what receives our subjective experience, but in a more objective sense, it does not exist at all.

Implications

The implications of all this, are that we have to live in the reality we perceive, while understanding it is an illusion of sorts. We must keep in mind what is actually real, while living what seems to be real.

That is why, from a moral perspective, the experience of people, moment by moment, in life, is what is important. That is something that is real for each person. These other ideas of strength and deserving, and all that crap mean nothing.

To base the quality of a person's life experience on criteria that they had no control over is nonsense. No one thinks a person born without the ability to provide for themselves should just be left to die. Yet other criteria are the result of things no one can control also. They are just a more complex series of events.

We can never escape the illusion entirely. We will continue to do things that ultimately make no sense at all, but we should at least understand they make no sense. We should also keep this in mind whenever possible.

From a practical perspective, we cannot help all people with all things. That is another reason we are stuck in the illusion. However, we can have compassion and understanding by recognizing the illusion.

My Philosophy

My philosophy takes all this sort of thing into account. There are many things we do not know, cannot know, or that cannot exist at all. Much of what we experience as reality, we create for ourselves, because in an objective sense, those things are all blank. From meta-ethics, to meaning, to purpose, and more.

Reality is a balance of chaos and order. It is the order of the laws of physics, but because of the complexity, our limited perspective, and us having only a partial understanding, we see it and experience it as chaos.

Particle interactions happen just as they would be predicted, but in such huge amounts, they cannot be predicted. At our scale, these appear to be pure chaos. We must then make order out of this chaos, in real time, as we experience it.

You can express a lot of this by saying "shit happens". I do express it like that sometimes. For me, this is all part of being a materialist. That was a contradiction in LaVey's Satanism; it advocates materialism, yet individuals seem to be these magical things divorced from causal reality. We are just smart animals, yet we somehow have this god-like control over our circumstances and who we are.

That does not work for me. We are indeed just smart animals. We do not have control of shit. Our self, is for each of us, the most important thing and the center of our reality. However, as real and import as subjective experience is, it is largely illusion from the perspective of objective reality.

A moral philosophy that starts from nothing (because there is nothing), is superior because the experience of each individual can become the basis of it. Practicality notwithstanding, we should value the experience of each without regard for what ends up being arbitrary criteria, due to everything ultimately being reduced to chance.

People may say "yeah but LaVey pasted in this stuff he got from Rand, and this other stuff he got from Redbeard, and then wrote this stuff that was based on his influence from them and maybe just a touch of Nietzsche." I say "so what?" So what. It does not work with the more primary idea that the material world is all there is and we are just animals. It does not work with what we have learned about reality.

If one continues with this same rational idea of materialism, one ends up with what I have laid out here. Not some magical sounding bunkum about qualities we cannot possibly have, or circumstances under the control of no one.

Then people may also say some theistic or spiritual type of thing, and "evidence or GTFO" is about the only response needed there. I have no doubt they will offer something they refer to as "evidence". It will not be though. It will be the same tired nonsense we have all heard on repeat forever.

For me, the truly definitive parts of LaVey's Satanism are the materialist aspect, the physical, carnal nature of humanity as animal, and then some of the more subjective ideas that are out of scope for this essay.

The implications of those definitive aspects contradict other parts that seem more like add-on and filler. The implications of materialism make the Randian, social Darwinist aspects of the philosophy entirely pointless and arbitrary.

If one cares nothing for the life experiences of others, that is a choice one can make. However, do not dress it up with false language about virtues that cannot exist in the material world. I think that is why some either drift away from materialism or temper the social Darwinist aspects whenever possible.

I see Satan as a metaphor for humanity as it is (among other things). This should include recognizing that the basis of many value judgments we make regarding people are an illusion.

Broader applications

Human cultures in general are even more caught up in this illusion than the given examples in Satanic philosophy. Therefore, of course the illusion colors various philosophies to different degrees. The illusion is absolutely ubiquitous in human thought. Even those of us aware of it cannot escape it entirely.

This does not mean we ignore how people behave, and what people do is of no consequence. It just means we cannot assign value to it for the purpose of judging. By that, I do not even mean whether or not something is good based on our normative values. I only mean in a blame and credit kind of way.

With blame and credit, we can still acknowledge what is, such as a particular person doing a specific thing. We just cannot apply that to the intrinsic goodness or badness of a person in regards to what they deserve. We can keep it in mind for predictions of future behavior, but not to fill the value of a bogus concept like "deserving".

This sort of cultural evolution will not reach that stage until long after we are all gone. However, we can keep that in mind and apply it in contexts like philosophy. That is how I arrive at some of the philosophical positions I take in regard to normative values, secular ethics, moral actions, and value judgments.

Since we live in this illusion, we do have to act within its confines up to a certain point. For practical purposes, we may have to consider how people behave in regard to normative values. We may look to those who have achieved certain things to achieve other goals in the future. We cannot help but admire that.

One major component of LaVey's Satanism was the rejection of the arbitrary value judgments of society. There are certain virtues, particularly those based in Christian theology, which were rejected. LaVey noted how people disregarded those supposed virtues whenever expedient, but then pretended to always follow them, and hold others accountable for them.

I largely agree with LaVey on that. However, I think his fondness for Rand and his understandable dislike of Jesus freak hippy culture, that was a major factor in 1960's Christian thought, had a negative, undue influence on which concepts he rejected. That is an area where I disagree.

More importantly, I do not like the way that 'boot straps', 'responsibility for the responsible', and other meaningless conservative platitudes became replacement virtues. I see

Satanists worshiping those supposed virtues as an idol, the way jingoists fawn over the flag, or the way traditional society worships the traditional values Satanism rejects.

These virtues are of course ignored whenever expedient. Sometimes shit happens. Those who have been able to live as such have merely been fortunate. It is pointless to worship at the altar of social Darwinism while acknowledging the reality of materialism. Part of that philosophy is that the virtues of social Darwinism are as arbitrary as the traditional virtues they replace.

The ultimate irony is that the Randian ideas that make up part of LaVey's Satanism, have become political doctrine for the conservative Christians, whose past virtues LaVey had rejected. I consider that the endgame victory for LaVey. It is all worth it just for that. However, that is no reason to live it.

It is better to move on from there, and embrace the implications of materialism. Only the wellbeing of oneself, one's community, and humanity as a whole, can be the basis of virtue. It is a subjective replacement for something that does not objectively exist. Much like we do with morality or meaning and purpose.

Living in the illusion our brains fashion for us, out of reality, makes various attributes of life and existence seem objectively real. Satanism is the knowledge that it is an illusion. It is also creating these attributes of life and existence for ourselves. If there is any meaning to the self-deification trope (and it is mostly misunderstood and misapplied silliness), it is in creating these attributes.

Consciousness is an illusion created by the communication of complex parts of the human brain. It is not a metaphysical you, separate from your material brain. It is a brain knowing itself and being aware of its own inner workings.

Satanism is knowing there is no inherent morality in the universe. Our group survival dynamic supplies the conscience that was an evolutionary advantage. These feelings are the replacement that we use as the basis for our normative values and applied ethics.

Satanism is knowing there is no inherent meaning or purpose in life. It is also embracing the absurdity of existence, and creating our own meaning and purpose in our own lives. It is understanding that much of ourselves, our wills, and even causal reality, are illusory; not at all what they seem to be.

Satanism is understanding the illusion while living within it, and making the most of that life. That is where materialism and skepticism lead. Shit happens.

All in Your Head

Satanism is a philosophy that has many subjective parts to it. There are a few different reasons for that. The most obvious is because it is a combination of multiple philosophies that go together.

Another reason is that individualism is at the heart of Satanic philosophy. This lends itself well to customization of subjective criteria. The remaining primary reason is that the self is at the center of it in some way.

Typically, people see Satanism as selfishness or worshiping the self as a god. How figurative the latter is varies greatly from person to person. It is a little different from that in my philosophy.

I reject the idea of self-worship because it is a very silly metaphor making use of ridiculous concepts. It also becomes a focus of spiritualists and occultists, which are incompatible with this philosophy.

Selfishness just ends up being a misused idea that becomes an excuse for personal shortcomings. Given that selfless acts tend to be enjoyed or valued by the person doing them, or at least further a group survival or betterment goal, selfish and selfless become a philosophically meaningless dichotomy. Because it is meaningless in this way, only the more colloquial meaning regarding behavior remains. Hence its use to excuse a lack of aesthetic.

In my philosophy, the idea of the self at the center of everything is in regard to subjective experience. Individualism, the motivation directed from within, and the focus on the self are all about subjective experience.

Reality is what is objective, and is everything external to the mind. There is much focus on objective reality because it is the same for everyone. One's opinion does not alter the laws of physics. However, subjective experience is how we perceive everything. It is an individual point of view for each person.

All of reality is perceived through one's senses, whether it is direct or indirect via a means of communication, such as written or verbal language. The senses are experienced by the mind, part of which is subjective experience. This is part of your consciousness and is your experience of consciousness and the world you perceive around you.

Consciousness and the rest of the mind are the result of physical processes in the brain. Scientifically, we do not fully understand consciousness, so philosophically, one can only speak of consciousness from the perspective of experience.

Consciousness, the mind, and the processes in the brain that produce this are not what this is about. However, one should understand that subjective experience is part of that. In a way, it is an illusion created by our complex brains, but it is also how we experience everything.

There is nothing that is not impacted by one's point of view or experience. Since objective reality must be perceived through this, one can only have virtual certainty of empirical facts. Everything is also subject to cognitive biases. The mind must exist for one to have the subjective experience to perceive it, so we can be certain of that. The distinction of virtual certainty is just philosophical though, and does not impact how sure we can be of empirical data in practice.

There is a lot more to understand about these topics. They are only mentioned here briefly to illustrate how subjective experience is at the center of everything. This is the meaning of the self being the center of this philosophy. This makes ideas of the self, take on philosophical meaning and significance, rather than just being the idle, meaningless musings of edgelords.

This makes subjective parts of the philosophy fit in with individualism and being on the Left-Hand Path. This is defined as motivation and direction coming from within, rather than emulating external group behaviors and adopting motivation and direction from there. Joining only with those on the same path rather than molding one's views to fit an arbitrarily selected group.

Individualism has more opportunities for expression when one acknowledges a void instead of believing without evidence. This is not always the case as the wellbeing of humanity is a readily apparent source of normative values due to our evolved group survival instincts. However, the lack of any meaning or purpose to life allows a huge void that gives one the opportunity to create any sort of meaning and purpose one desires.

Embracing existential nihilism and the absurdity of existence gives one a blank canvas for life. If I may take the painting metaphor a step further, I will quote Bob Ross: "This is your world. You're the creator." Pick any purpose or purposes you wish, change them, and make them simple or complex with many parts. Do the same for meaning. This is where individualism comes in, as well as creativity.

The meaning of one's life certainly involves wit and humor, as well as pleasure and indulgence. I am certain those concepts are quite familiar. They are central pillars of Satanism. Pick your pleasures and indulge in them; laugh at the absurdity of life; Stare into the void with eager anticipation and a creative agenda. For you are a Satanist and live life on your own terms.

Your personal ideas of your meaning and purpose, combined with direction and motivation from within, along with your subjective experience of the natural world and your life, combine to fill the space some might label "God". Those who would call it that believe it is external, and that is partly indoctrination and partly because their right hand path motivation comes from outside. Call it what you will, but understand it is a metaphorical construct of the inner world of your mind. It is the self. Some might call it Satan, but it is only part of that larger metaphor.

It is still the self at the center of all. It is just a different way of looking at it; a more thought-out and rational way of looking at it. One must go beyond simplistic, dumbed-down interpretations like being a selfish edgelord, emulating expected in-group behaviors. The self is all the things I laid out. It is the answer to the void, and it is all in your head.

Abortion: A Satanic Perspective

The context of this essay was events in late 2017 and early 2018. It is the same as the version posted on the website, but with a little more added to the end.

Also, note that it is not just cis women who can become pregnant. There are trans men who still have a uterus, and some nonbinary people. Hence my use of more inclusive language.

With recent news both good and bad, abortion has been on the minds of many, myself included. In Missouri, the abortion restrictions are being challenged in a case being heard by the state Supreme Court. In bad news on the national level, a twenty-week ban has been proposed.

I am going to explain here why I have come to a few conclusions. First, that while abortion affects women, trans men, nonbinary people assigned female at birth, and anyone else who can become pregnant, far more, it is an issue for everyone, even gay and asexual men. Second, that it seeks to enforce a religious opinion upon women. Third, that it violates the first amendment rights of everyone. Finally, that it amounts to the state telling people what they must think. This means that there can be no wavering on this issue.

Frequently in debates, people want to conflate what "life" means. Life in general, as in just being alive is conflated with sentient life. Everything with human DNA is human, and sex cells are alive long before they ever join, and all the ones that never join are alive at some point. Despite the conflation, we only mean sentience.

There are no facts as to when human life reaches the point of sentience. In science, there is no point where sentience "happens". We can be nearly certain that it is sentient when it is viable, and it being a separate life dependent on no other for a life support system, makes it a moot point at that stage anyway. However, prior to that point, there are not any actual facts about when it becomes a person.

The beginning of life is a religious opinion. Various religions have all sorts of different opinions on when life begins. Some religions believe in a soul, and think it joins with the body at one stage or another. Other religions do not believe in souls, and look to brain development.

While the total lack of a religion is not a religion, it is an opinion that religion is unnecessary. So even people like that have a religious opinion of sorts, that being that the views of organized groups have no bearing on their opinions.

With the beginning of life being a matter of opinion, there can be no mandate on non-viable fetuses, or human tissue of earlier stages. Everyone has a right to their opinion, and the opinion of all must be respected.

If one is opposed to abortion, then it is their right to not even consider abortion during their pregnancy. If someone feels abortion is acceptable up to a certain point, then they should be able to do that. If someone feels it is all right at any point, that should be fine as well.

This is simplified to choice. As life is a religious opinion, and everyone has freedom of religion and a right to their opinion, each given person should be able to decide what to do about a pregnancy. Any restriction on abortion is a denial of religious opinion, in favor of a state-mandated religious opinion.

Abortion, like birth control, is part of family planning. When people are going to have children, decisions about when to have them, and how to plan a family, are deeply personal opinions. Sometimes these views may be religious or cultural, but they are always personal. Any abortion restriction amounts to the state enforcing a family planning opinion. They are saying that your family planning must have a chance of random children in the event of unintended conception.

The decision of whether or not to have children at all is a personal decision, and a matter of opinion. Abortion restrictions are telling you that you must accept a chance of having children, regardless of your opinion on that matter. One should be entitled to their own opinion, as we are in all other personal matters, whether or not one ever has any children.

The meaning and significance of sex and sexuality are usually the most personal opinions one has. They are sometimes cultural and/or religious as well. Some people may see it as sacred, only for couples to have kids, and that it involves the approval of a deity, some see it as nothing but a biological function, and a multitude of opinions lie in between.

Abortion restrictions are always predicated on one accepting a chance of children when engaging in sexual activity. It is frequently stated that people should not have sex at all if they do not want children. This not only dictates sexual behavior, but also the significance and meaning one must place on sex and sexuality.

We cannot allow any restrictions at all on abortion because of the bodily autonomy of women and others who can become pregnant. Even if one does not care about others, it is still important, even for gay and asexual men.

When abortion is restricted in any way, the state is mandating a few different opinions. It is saying that life begins at conception or other point they have determined, that family planning must allow for children from unintended pregnancies, that any sexual activity must have some chance of children, that abstaining from sex is the only way not to have children, that sex carries a minimum level of significance and meaning.

Abortion restrictions are ultimately a state-mandate on what we think regarding our most personal opinions. While it is not possible to directly mandate thought, abortion restrictions are predicated on beliefs, which are all opinions, all deeply personal in nature, and the effects of which are identical to that of people who share those state-mandated beliefs.

By being forced to act in accordance with a set of state-mandated beliefs, our beliefs on those points are being overridden. Usually laws are not entirely devoid of all objective fact, whether right or wrong, and based entirely on opinions. In no other case are laws based on nothing but opinions, when all the opinions are religious, cultural, and personal, and ones that are so deeply held.

With choice everyone has a right to their opinion, and their own beliefs about the most personal elements of one's life. Any restriction to that is the state dictating what the beliefs of everyone must be. Lawmakers and lobbyists are legislating their religious beliefs, forcing them off on all of us.

Those who can become pregnant bear the greatest burden, as it is an assault on their bodily autonomy. It is also an assault on our most personal beliefs about the beginning of life, and the significance and meaning of sex and sexuality.

Even if you just consider people who favor some sort of abortion restriction, what they are saying is that their opinion should override the opinions of other people. They are for the state forcing other people to live as if they share those opinions, regardless of the opinions held by everyone else.

I am not going to "respect" the opinion of someone, when that opinion, is that their opinions on the most deeply personal matters must override the opinions of everyone else, via a state mandate. They are saying they think everyone else must be forced to live as if they share opinions contrary to the ones they actually have.

If someone has no respect for the most personal beliefs of others, and thinks the state should force them to live in accordance with different beliefs, on matters that are entirely subjective, with no objective component at all, then I have no reason to respect any of their opinions at all. I also refuse to accept a view that some group of people does not get the same level of bodily autonomy.

Any views favoring any abortion restrictions are an opinion against the most fundamental human rights of others. It is a view that some get less bodily autonomy than others, and that everyone must live as if they accept a set of fundamental beliefs about life, sexuality, and the very essence of what it is to be human, that contradict the beliefs they actually hold.

Additional Thoughts

The abortion issue being so contentious has nothing to do with aborting fetuses. It is about the fundamental beliefs we have about what it is to be human, and the meaning of life. One group of people feels that everyone has a set of beliefs and their own understanding of what it means to be human, and what the meaning of life is.

Another group of people feels that the existence of opinions outside a particular range, regarding what it means to be human and the meaning of life, are intolerable, as such beliefs are an offense to their concept of life and to their deity, who allegedly shares that view. They feel the remedy is to force all others into behaviors consistent with their acceptable range of beliefs on the aforementioned things.

For Completeness

For the sake of completeness, it is worth circling back to another point I did not work into the essay. This is more typically where I go when arguing on this topic, but I wanted to get right into the points I planned on digging into.

In no other circumstance, can the body of one person be used to keep another person alive. Without consent, you cannot take organs or even blood from someone, even if it saves the life of another.

Without consent, you cannot even take blood or organs from a corpse, even to save a living person. So by that standard, you do not even need to get into points about religious opinion. The only reason I did was because people who want to override the opinions of others, always demand respect for their opinion that other people do not get an opinion.

What it is actually about

Abortion restrictions, for those who want to legislate them, are about religious and cultural supremacy. For Christian supremacists, who also seek to enforce their Victorian-lite culture, controlling women, their bodies, their sexuality, their reproductive choices, their most personal beliefs, and everything about them, is of primary importance. Such an authoritarian, patriarchal culture is most threatened by women and their autonomy.

Freedom and equality for women is in direct opposition to the hegemonic power of these religious and cultural supremacists. That is why they fight so hard against women, and any group that champions the rights of women. They seem to be even more threatened by that than they are of people with opposing religious beliefs.

People like that are ultimately seeking mind control. They want all thought to be identical to their own with no dissension. Any people who wish to have any amount of freedom must oppose them at every turn and give no ground at all. Not one inch. The bodily autonomy of those who can become pregnant is the front line of this fight. We must be resolute in the defense of that.

𝔉𝔯𝔢𝔢 𝔖𝔭𝔢𝔢𝔠𝔥 𝔦𝔰𝔰𝔲𝔢𝔰

*This is from a Facebook post where I address the free
speech debates that had been going on in 2017 and 2018 in
some Satanism circles on social media. There were certain
factions that took an absolutist stance on free speech, seemed
lacking in knowledge, and extremely overconfident about their
understanding. I have a very different view on this topic.*

I take issue with free speech absolutism and I take even
more issue with this particular form of free speech absolutism,
which is invariably the form it takes every single time.

Remember when Milo Ynnopoulis did not get to speak at a
college? Oh, the echoing cries of white neoliberals and
libertarians, and all the tears, just barrels of tears. Because if

colleges do not give him a venue, how else will his views be heard, other than the books he authored and all the time he spent as an editor for Breitbart?

We got similar reactions about Richard Spencer too, who went so far as to advocate for a white ethno state and ethnic cleansing. Oh his speech! If he cannot speak then liberal democracy -- nay, civilization, as we know it, will surly collapse.

When people take an absolutist position on free speech, it is hard to say which legal exceptions they will see as valid. Some see little to none as valid. There are some who will go through the mental gymnastics to convince themselves that defamation is perfectly all right. There are some that accept all legal exceptions. Those people, while avoiding some mental contortions, are implying, and will sometimes explicitly state, that those are fine and no other limitations are valid. It is a spectrum.

What they all have in common is that they think legally defining free speech is all cut and dry; that it is so simple and easy. It is as if there have not been a fuckload of cases about it with all sorts of legal opinions from all sorts of brilliant legal scholars. It is as if the question of free speech has not been debated for somewhere around 2500 years.

We should be so glad to have their brilliant minds, to impart their absolute certainty to us, that there can be no other limits on free speech than what they say.

Moving beyond that, let's address violence and threats of violence specifically. Because, let's be honest here, the issue is always a white man saying something that one or more other groups see as threatening.

The argument is usually minority groups and leftists saying some asshole does not get to organize a rally around building a political movement with a platform of ethnic cleansing.

White male free speech absolutists swoop in like superman to defend said asshole's right to speak and recruit other Nazis or whatever is going on.

The first group says it is not speech because it is threatening violence, and the other bunch of course says that it is not threatening violence. In fact, they insist that speech cannot contain inherent violence. Or rather, in their "confidence", they say it as a strawman like "speech is not violence" and even write stupid articles about it because obviously those silly minorities think words equal punching.

Or who knows, maybe it is an unintentional strawman, and really their understanding of the argument they are responding to is as simplistic and sophomoric as their understanding of free speech and its legal limits.

The white guys of course do not see any of the stuff said as threatening at all. But why would they? It does not threaten them. They have nothing to fear at all.

For people who are racial minorities or transgender, for example, it can seem quite threatening. People who want to exterminate them are taking the first steps of realizing their goals, politically. There can be exceptions, but many of those individuals do feel threatened.

In addition, it sets up a situation where those views become more normalized, and makes a more hostile environment for various minority groups. Take Trump's rise to power for example. You cannot deny the racism and xenophobia that has been brought to the surface. That is violence, and it is still a far cry from Spencer. These sorts of views have been cited by plenty of gunman (who are not crazy) as the grievances that motivated their actions.

As white people, I do not think we really get to tell people of color which threats are sufficiently threatening and which are not.

What really makes me go "WTF?!" is when I notice someone arguing free speech absolutism who will claim anything and everything angrily said to them is a threat.

You would also think that free speech absolutists would be championing black football players who want to take a knee during the national anthem. They are strangely silent on it. I am sure somewhere out there is a free speech absolutist who mentioned it once, but for the most part, nothing.

I do not think these people are taking this position to be intentionally malicious. I think it is 100% a problem of perspective. They do not understand all the complexity in what is and is not free speech. They do not see the things people are pointing out as threats, to be threatening. These are all common biases in thinking.

Believing you fully understand something when actually you do not know enough to realize how little you know is a common bias. Being biased in favor of people in one's own demographic is a common bias. Judging threats (and other things) based only on one's own perspective is yet another common bias. Seeing everything as two equal sides is another common bias, at least in our current culture anyway. It is not something innate to all humans like the other biases though.

What is really ironic is that those biases play major roles in Christians wanting only their religion in the public sphere and not one like, oh I don't know... Satanism, for example. Obviously, that is only ironic for some free speech absolutists, not the majority of them. As some free speech absolutists are those Christians. Therefore, it is very consistent for some.

So where are the lines of what is and is not speech you ask? Well, I think things like ethnic cleansing fall outside of it, and I think inherent violence, or anything with an action component is not speech. But in determining where the demarcation point is for these various criteria... I do not know. It will take people with far more knowledge than I to determine extremely complicated things like that. Legal scholars and philosophers will almost certainly still be debating that long after I am dead and gone, perhaps for another 2500 years.

Importance and Priorities

Philosophies tend to impact many ideas, ways of thinking, and potential sets of actions. When taken as a collection, the impact spans one's entire worldview. Such is the way with Satanism, as it is a collection of philosophies. There are many different variations too. It also varies from person to person, even within a specific variation. Or at least it should if all is well with a given variation.

For me, and the variation I created, there are some important points; things that spill over into life like an overflowing cup. These are areas of greater importance; things that should be priorities.

One major category is self-determination. This should be both in thought and in action. One's thoughts will in turn drive one's actions. The starting point is thinking for yourself.

Being told what to think, as in an imperative, should be a warning sign, giving fright to any rational person. This is not the same as being provided information though. One can derive knowledge from such information, given proper evaluation. With the right methodology, such knowledge leads to beliefs about objective facts that are true. It can also be part of the basis for one's subjective views.

Being told what to think, when accepted without question, will lead to beliefs that may be false, and serve only the interests of the one giving the order. You have your own interests to consider, which should be your priority. You also have objective reality to contend with. No one and nothing will ever change reality. The laws of physics do not care what anyone thinks. Understanding reality is important.

A major theme for me is providing information and guidance while never telling anyone what to think. Individuals must decide on this for themselves. Never listen to those who demand you think a certain way, or believe certain things.

I may have certain criteria for who can be a member of an organization due to the definition of the organization and its members. Therefore, I am particular about that. I also do not solicit people to join up and/or try to push the philosophical criteria off on anyone. I believe that one must make such a choice entirely free of pressure, based on one's own research.

The criteria is preexisting. Nothing gets sprung on people after the fact. It is all laid out for everyone to read too. I even require that people attest that they have read and understood my philosophy. That is how important that is to me. People who do not understand can only join if they have lied to me about their understanding. That is a choice they made.

That is what I believe to be the correct scenario. That is not a typical methodology though. Not everyone has their information up front. Not everyone checks for understanding. There may be places that make demands on what one believes after the fact too.

This is not just confined to Satanism, or even to religion in general. You may encounter those who tell you things after the fact, after having presented only minimal information about the group in question, in any context or area of life at all. You may be told to accept things without question. You may be told to believe things with no good reason provided.

I would advise never giving up any piece of your autonomy for anyone. Actions require motivating reason.

Action on demand in the absence of such reason is a sign of tyranny.

For me, Satan is a metaphor of personal autonomy and rebellion against any oppressive authority. Satan is thinking for oneself and not bowing to arbitrary demands of any authority figure.

It is perfectly fine for one to have certain rules in regard to one's property, and the use thereof. You would not let someone borrow something of yours if they damage that property or otherwise take advantage of your generosity. However, when a dictatorial figure uses ownership of a given thing as a Trojan Horse to dictating your belief and/or action, one should exit the situation to maintain their autonomy. One's autonomy is too great a price to pay for any carrot held out for the purpose of the acceptance of dictatorial demand.

One may now ask, when evaluating anything, as is required for independent thought, "what are the components and the methodology?" That is an excellent question, and the answer is a complex one. The answer brings me back around to other things that are priorities. These are knowledge, belief, and the relationship thereof.

Knowledge is the starting point, which then informs belief. That is how one evaluates any objective claim. When one asks you to accept a belief that is vague and has no evidence, you are being asked to accept a belief without the prerequisite knowledge to know it is true. When there is an implied action or actions that go along with this belief the motivations become clear. It is best to reject it outright. All objective, empirical claims require empirical evidence to be accepted.

When a given thing is true, in an objective sense, there is knowledge forming the basis of this belief. The data must be verified by logic in the case of reason, or by peer reviewed studies in the case of empirical data. Usually these things will be combined.

Firsthand empirical knowledge, such as from one's senses is acceptable too. Just keep in mind that different types of claims require different levels of verification. Sometimes it is a simple thing and you just need to see it. Other times it may be something that overturns a conventional understanding of science, in which case careful evaluation of peer reviewed studies is required.

The evaluated knowledge can then inform belief through the application of logical reasoning. One must take care to avoid logical fallacies when doing this. When that has been done, you can have a belief of some sort.

Unfounded beliefs are problematic and must be avoided. In addition to a plethora of other problems, unfounded beliefs lead one to being manipulated by others. This makes one vulnerable to the interests of others, which may likely run counter to one's own. Frequently they run counter to the interests of humanity in general.

In addition to avoiding unfounded beliefs and having only valid ones, informed by verified knowledge, value judgments are also a major priority. This gets into moral philosophy.

The moral feelings one thinks of as conscience, come into play with knowledge and belief when thinking critically. These feelings then have reason applied in order to guide one's decisions and actions.

In this process, one must be free of arbitrary values. They cloud your judgment. One must not have any beliefs of an objective nature, which are false. This is where your conscience will point you in the wrong direction due to being wrong about some aspect of reality.

If one has a false belief due to some factor like a presupposed cultural belief, one may come to an incorrect conclusion in the evaluation of an ethical consideration. Is the idea presupposed on the basis of a societal factor, or is the idea a belief that has been informed by knowledge? Where did you get this idea? How do you know this? Follow it to its source.

Do not be afraid of being wrong. Do not crave being right. Being wrong is an opportunity to increase one's knowledge. Celebrate being wrong! Celebrate your area of ignorance! Rejoice in filling that ignorance with knowledge! One can only take pride in being right, when one has the knowledge to justify such a belief.

Understanding the need to obtain a given piece of knowledge can come from being wrong. There are plenty of ways one can gain an understanding of a need to obtain knowledge. However, being wrong always leads there. Even if the ultimate answer is that you do not know, you still end up being right at the end of the process.

When one has the feelings of conscience and the beliefs informed by knowledge, free of bias, it is possible to make moral decisions based on the feelings of conscience. In an absence of any entirely objective basis, this is the best that can be done. This is another priority.

Sometimes one may be asked to do things that violate the feelings of conscience. Fallacious reasoning may be given to assuage the resulting feelings or even no reason at all. The conscience can be initially wrong, but given appropriate data and reasoning, one can conform to these feelings without subverting them through the loophole of fallacy.

Being asked to do and think things that are unethical, by these criteria, should be a warning sign. There are other interests at work here. Such nonsense should be rejected. Do not follow orders. Think for yourself.

Various forces can be brought to bear when one is uncooperative due to following the above guidelines. When these pressures are used to subvert your reasoning, you know that it is time to flee. There should always be a reason. Never blindly follow someone.

The wellbeing of yourself and of humanity are of prime importance. They are priorities. Satanism should have a methodology of that wellbeing as a minimum, in addition to all the bits of philosophical icing on this metaphorical cake.

A Community by Any Other Name

Community is a concept where there is a lot of disagreement on the surface, but it is more a matter of definition and criteria than people seeing it differently.

Within Satanism, the community concept actually hinges on what Satanism is in total compared to what a given type of Satanism is. This varies greatly of course.

The Church of Satan maintains that a Satanic community is impossible. While my general sentiment is one of disagreement, if I were to take their definition of Satanism as a given, I would agree. As their view is that their Satanism is the only Satanism, and their view of this is also quite broad, such a community is impossible.

Within the Satanic milieu, the definition of Satanism in total is very broad. It is much wider than the Church of Satan's view. However, these organizations have a concept of "our Satanism". That is usually narrower than how the Church of Satan sees it. There are exceptions though.

Members of the Church of Satan do belong to communities, and do participate in activism. These are outside interests though. However, I do not think any CoS member would claim that the presence of more than one Satanist within a charity would destroy said charity. I do not think it is like The Highlander where there can be only one.

You could theoretically have a group that was essentially Church of Satan members who are liberal and participate in pro-choice activism. This is an extremely simplistic example. It illustrates the point though. It can be a type of community. They do not see it as a Satanic one though because it does not define their type of Satanism. Because there are no "types of Satanism" as far as they are concerned, there can be no Satanic community. I agree. Defined as such, a Satanic community is impossible.

While there is nothing so simplistic as a "CoS philosophy plus liberalism and pro-choice activism" type of Satanism, there are organizations as narrowly defined.

Activism tends to be what people focus on with community, but that is a red herring. That is just one possible element. The reason that is the focus is because The Satanic Temple focuses on that, and they are the next largest organization after the Church of Satan.

While The Satanic Temple has this community component, what that means is just as nebulous as every other aspect of TST due to their lack of any cohesive philosophy. There are the tenets and some selections of classic literature where the reader simply extrapolates whatever they wish to make of that based on their interpretation, but nothing beyond that.

Arguments regarding the meaning of the tenets will demonstrate well that each given person brings a lot of previously made conclusions to the table. Therefore, the common activism activities are what defines their sense of community, and in conjunction with the tenets, the organization in total.

In the case of the United Aspects of Satan, community is more defined around those who share the philosophy of Ba'alian Satanism. Ba'alian Satanism is the UAoS concept of "our Satanism". It is very narrowly defined. It is a very small piece of what Satanism is in total. That makes community possible.

When comparing LaVeyan Satanism to Ba'alian Satanism, the focus is usually on the differences in general. There are many things that the two philosophies have in common though. As Ba'alian Satanism is much more narrow, the piece of it that falls outside LaVeyan Satanism is relatively small. However, there is quite a lot of LaVeyan Satanism that falls outside of Ba'alian Satanism.

This is because LaVey defined Satanism in its entirety, and therefore in very broad terms. Everyone who came after wanted to make a variation. Usually they were more narrow, some falling entirely within LaVey's definition, many others veering outside of that to varying degrees.

As the UAoS defines its type of Satanism, community is certainly possible. Individualism remains intact too, because of this narrow set of criteria, laid out in The Satanic Narratives. It is not meant for everyone. People who happen to share it just come together under that shared philosophy.

The UAoS (at least in this way) is no different from the very simplistic example of "Church of Satan members who are liberal and participate in pro-choice activism". In the view of the Church of Satan, neither is a distinct type of Satanism. This means the aspect of community and the Satanism part stay entirely separate in their view.

LaVey made his Satanism to be inclusive to a certain extent, although very much exclusive in other ways. My type of Satanism was made with a very different purpose. Rather than defining Satanism in general, I simply defined my path. There are other people on this path too, but relatively few. Being a potential UAoS member is a very specific thing.

The specificity of my philosophy, and how very particular I am about it, is one of many reasons I support independent organizations. Maybe they are not exactly on my path, but it is close. Close enough that they can take a slightly modified version of my philosophy and use it to define their own path. They can also center it around issues important to the local area they are in.

You can also have local communities that have a UAoS member or two, along with some Satanists who are just very similar. They have enough in common with the local goals to form their own community together. They are individualists uniting in common cause. This is no different from the aforementioned example of specific CoS members.

This is why differences in views on community are really just differences in how one defines Satanism and their own type of Satanism. If my type of Satanism were as broad as LaVey's, I would not see community and individualism as being compatible either.

Do not get me wrong, LaVey's Satanism is very much flavored by his personal path. Just look at the Rand influence within it, for example. Nevertheless, in other ways, it is very broad, which was his intent. Mine was all about my path, partly because it was mine, and partly because I knew many others were on that path too. I stated that intent in The Satanic Narratives, just as LaVey laid out his intent in The Satanic Bible.

It is not that the concept of community is viewed differently. It is just how you define a given type of Satanism that determines if it is possible. Therefore, arguments about the possibility of a Satanic community are nearly always the result of having differing definitions of Satanism.

An understanding of what the other side is saying becomes impossible for each side. That discussion falls back on the meaning of Satanism. That is the impasse for everything, as some people do not recognize the concept of variations.

This is the nature of philosophy in general. It branches off into variations. Something like Satanism, which is a collection of philosophies, is going to be even more like that than an individual philosophy. These different variations are going to have different aspects, which may be compatible in some ways, but not compatible in others.

Saying a particular concept generally works or is entirely impossible in one's own philosophy says nothing of its compatibility or lack thereof in a similar philosophy. That is all these community discussions are.

(

Epilogue

This fills in some additional details in the philosophy. If you go back and read The Satanic Narratives, you will notice I mentioned many of these ideas. It was a very accessible book for people who were not very familiar with philosophy. For those who had read a lot of philosophy, you could get it on another level. Those are the details I went over here.

There are, of course, many more details. I have long been planning a large philosophy book to go over all of it. However, that book will be a long time in the making. Writing these essays will help me figure out what all should be in it.

Until then, I will continue adding to the websites. I will also post my ideas on social media, in addition to my less serious posts. As always, I enjoy hearing from all of you there.

Hail Satan!

About the Author

Damien Ba'al is a technology professional by day and a philosopher by night. He is a Satanist, a skeptic, a critical thinker, and many other things. Damien lives with his wife and cats, where he enjoys a number of intellectual hobbies. He has a love of learning and of teaching. Active on social media, Damien's words convey his dark presence to all the outcasts and individualists traveling the Left-Hand Path.

https://www.facebook.com/author.damien.baal

https://twitter.com/Damien_Baal @Damien_baal

http://damienbaal.com/

http://uaofsatan.org/

http://atheisticsatanism.com/

Also by Damien Ba'al

The Satanic Narratives: A Modern Satanic Bible*

United Aspects of Satan: The Black Book

The Satanic Praxis: Living the Narratives

Also available in Spanish

Shit Happens

Implications of Physicalism in Satanic Philosophy

Published by Skeptic

an imprint of HLA Publishing LLC

hlapublishing.com

ISBN: 978-0-9986198-3-5

www.ingramcontent.com/pod-product-compliance
Lightning Source LLC
Chambersburg PA
CBHW071621040426
42452CB00009B/1422